PANDEMIC BUDGETING & FINANCES

How to Use Piggy Banks and Stop Counting Sheep

RESHMA BHOJWANI

Pandemic Budgeting & Finances

ISBN: 978-1-943515-37-0

AcuteByDesign, Publisher

Printed in the United States of America

AcuteByDesign
the little book company that could
A Michael Marion Sharpe Company

Michele Thomas,
Executive Publisher

Dedication

To all who have been affected by the pandemic in some shape or form, we are in this together and this too shall pass. When it does, we will emerge stronger, more empowered, and more united than ever before.

Very best wishes,

Reshma Bhojwani

Contents

Introduction

Pandemic Crisis, Bring It On!

It was the first of the month, and my mortgage payment was due. I am usually always on top of things when it comes to my finances and paying my bills on time, but July 1, 2015, was not an ordinary day in my life.

My stomach was in knots as I waited for the judge to review the documents and the settlement agreement that my husband and I had signed, and submitted to the court. Connecticut requires that a hearing be held before a judge grants an uncontested divorce. After what seemed like an eternity, the judge asked us some questions and continued reviewing the documents. I breathed a sigh of relief when he finally accepted our divorce agreement and asked us to collect our divorce decree from the court.

I had spent all day at the courthouse and, as you can imagine, the day had been an emotional roller coaster for me; even after I got home, it was far from over. In the past, having been embarrassed a couple of times due to my checks bouncing, because of insufficient funds (never intentionally, of course), I had gotten into the habit of confirming that I had enough money in my bank account before writing a check. When I needed to write one to the mortgage company, I logged into my bank account and was horrified to see that I was short by $600.

My husband at that time got paid every first and fifteenth of the month and his company did a direct deposit. However, even though it was the first of the month, there was no money deposited. That is when reality kicked in, and I began to shake like a leaf. Now he was no longer my husband, and his money was no longer my money. Over the years, we take certain things for granted, like our husband's money. In the aftermath of the divorce, I had gone from two incomes to one overnight, which meant I could no longer afford my mortgage payment.

My mind began racing – where was I going to get the $600? How was I going to pay the mortgage this month? Would I have a roof over my head next month? What else couldn't I afford? Then came self-doubt; was getting a divorce a bad decision? Did I rush into it? Would I be able to manage everything by myself? By that time, I was a bundle of nerves, and tears were rolling down my cheeks.

As I sat there crying, holding the mortgage bill in my hand, I knew I had to pull myself together and come up with the $600 as soon as possible. This wasn't the time for self-pity, and I had to learn to face the new reality of my life. I said to myself, I could do this; it was just another crisis and it would pass. I had been in a crisis before and survived when I became unemployed during the 2008 recession, and we had to live off of only my husband's income, so why was this any different? I took a deep breath and immediately felt my body relaxing.

Because of my ex-husband's bad money-spending habits, we had been spending more money than we were bringing in, but now that he was gone, I could fix that. I realized I had to go full throttle and put an emergency budget together immediately: not just a **budget**, but a **"pandemic" emergency budget.**

Now you must be wondering, has she lost her mind? What on earth is a pandemic emergency budget? Be it a crisis due to unemployment, recession, divorce, or the coronavirus pandemic, a crisis is a crisis and you need to switch to an **emergency budget** immediately. We will be referring to a "crisis", as a "pandemic crisis" in this book.

> A **budget** is an estimate of income and expenditures for a set period of time.
>
> An **emergency budget** is a **budget** that you set up when you need to cut out ALL unnecessary expenses in order to survive during a pandemic crisis. It is something that you should have in place as soon as possible, as emergencies don't wait for you to get prepared, before they occur.

Chapter 1

Budgeting During Good Times and Bad

Before my divorce, even though I tracked my income and expenses in a spreadsheet and tallied the numbers with the bank statement every month, I hadn't really created a written budget; but after the divorce, I buckled down and created an emergency budget right away. In order to survive and still have a roof over my head, I was left with no other choice but to drastically reduce my expenses and find creative ways to increase my income simultaneously. I explain how I did that in Chapter 2.

Thankfully, unlike my ex-husband, I was a saver and not a spender. Despite my single income, with a few tweaks to the expenses, I was able to create a new lifestyle without making too many sacrifices and still live within my means. It goes without saying that creating an emergency budget was the key factor, without which I would have continued hurting financially. Emergency budgeting gave me peace of mind.

Once I was comfortable with my financial situation and capable of affording all my expenses, I switched to creating a budget, planning for my future, focusing on building my emergency fund, and paying off my debts. Did I tell you about the $25,000 debt I got stuck with during the settlement agreement, thanks to my ex-husband's bad money-spending habits? I can't wait to tell you more about that and how I paid it off in less than three years in Chapter 3.

I can tell from firsthand experiences that budgeting and emergency budgeting are extremely powerful tools. It helped me during my divorce and is definitely helping me now during the coronavirus pandemic of 2020, so please don't just read about it and put this book away on your shelf before you take action. You can keep it simple; you don't need to overthink it.

Tip For Budgeting During A Pandemic Crisis

Tip

If you don't already have a budget in place, start with creating an emergency budget and then switch to a budget when you are in a better financial situation.

If you already have a budget, then either switch to an emergency budget or tweak your budget as per your financial situation.

What do you need to do differently when creating a budget versus an emergency budget?

Budget	Emergency Budget
Plan and manage your expenses	Cut all your unnecessary expenses immediately
Build and grow your emergency fund	Use your emergency fund sparingly. If you don't have any, then build one first
Save toward your goals, like vacations, car maintenance and repair, etc.	Hold off on saving toward goals and put those funds into your emergency fund
Pay off your debts as quickly as possible	Pay only the minimum payment due on your debts if you can't afford to pay more
Build and grow your retirement fund as much as possible	To generate more income, reduce your retirement contribution temporarily; if you don't have any, then sell unwanted things from your house

Some examples of how you can start building your emergency fund during a pandemic crisis:

Reduce expenses	**Tax-return money**	**Stimulus check**
Sell unwanted things from home	**Reduce retirement contribution temporarily**	**Hold off on saving for goals like vacation**

Example of a budget versus an emergency budget:

BUDGET	EMERGENCY BUDGET
Income - $2000	Income - $2000
Expenses	Expenses
Mortgage or Rent - $1000	Mortgage or Rent - $1000
House maintenance - $50	House maintenance - $25
Electricity - $90	Electricity - $75
Cable/Internet - $100	Cable/Internet - $80
Cell - $75	Cell - $75
Car loan - $200	Car loan - $200
Auto Insurance - $50	Auto Insurance - $50
Gas - $60	Gas - $30
Grocery - $150	Grocery - $120
Restaurant - $50	Restaurant - $0
Clothes - $50	Clothes - $0
Gifts - $60	Gifts - $0
Misc - $65	Misc - $20
Total Expense = $2000	Total Expense = $1675

As you can see above, in the emergency budget, all the unnecessary expenses have been cut down to the bare bones, and the other expenses have been reduced by a total of $325.

To put this in perspective:

For those who do not have an emergency fund, you would now be able to start putting $325 a month toward it.

For those who do have an emergency fund, your funds would last longer.

To further illustrate how this would work, if your income got cut in half to $1,000 (as per example) during the pandemic crisis and you had $5,000 in your emergency fund:

BUDGET	EMERGENCY BUDGET
Income - $1000 (cut in half)	Income - $1000 (cut in half)
Expense - $2000	Expense - $1675
Money shortage - $1000	Money shortage - $675
Emergency Fund - $5000	Emergency Fund - $5000
$5000/$1000 = 5	$5000/$675 = 7.4
Your emergency funds will last for 5 months	Your emergency funds will last for 7 months

As you can see above, by having a budget in place, your emergency funds would last for five months, but with an emergency budget in place, the same amount of money would last for seven months, meaning you could weather the storm for an additional two months during the pandemic crisis.

Now that you understand the significance of a budget and an emergency budget, let's take a deeper dive in the next chapter on how you can increase your income and decrease your expenses. But first, before we proceed, make sure you have created a written budget or an emergency budget depending on your current financial situation.

Action Steps to Create a Budget

1) Write down your income and expenses.
2) Create a budget and/or an emergency budget.
3) Calculate your money shortage (if any).
4) Calculate how long your emergency fund will last, if you have one.

Chapter 2

Do You Want to Be at the Top of the Seesaw or the Bottom?

My first night after the divorce was finalized, I stared at the ceiling all night long, haunted by the question of how I was going to get the additional $600 to pay my mortgage bill that month. I had to go to work the next day, and was desperately trying to get some sleep. I was exhausted from spending all day at the courthouse, but my mind wouldn't let me sleep. As I tossed and turned, it dawned on me that I no longer had a grip on what my cash flow looked like with my new financial situation. With some of my ex-husband's expenses gone, I was clueless about how much money was going out, as compared to the new amount coming in.

Just the thought of no longer knowing my numbers frightened me, and I bolted up in bed, startled.

I immediately got out from underneath the covers, jumped out of bed, grabbed a piece of paper and a pen, scribbled all the expenses I could think of, and added them up. Then I jotted down my **net income**, which is my take-home pay. When I subtracted my expenses from my take-home pay, I realized that I was short by $1,000, out of which $600 was for the mortgage payment; but what about the remaining $400? What other bills could I not afford? By the time I was done, I was wide awake and, since it was no use trying to go back to bed, I went to the kitchen and made myself a cup of chamomile tea in the hope of calming down and getting some sleep for a couple of hours. At that point I was ready to try anything.

Tip

When your financial situation changes, be it an increase or a decrease in income, get acquainted with your new numbers immediately. Take a piece of paper and pencil and jot down your income and expenses. Use the KISS principle (keep it simple, stupid). You like that, huh? 😊

Would you rather check if you have gas in your car before you start driving or wait until you come to a screeching halt because you ran out of gas?

So why do you treat money any differently? By tracking your income and expenses, all you are doing is planning what you are going to do with your money before you start spending it, versus coming to a screeching halt because you ran out of money.

Managing your money (Proactive Approach)

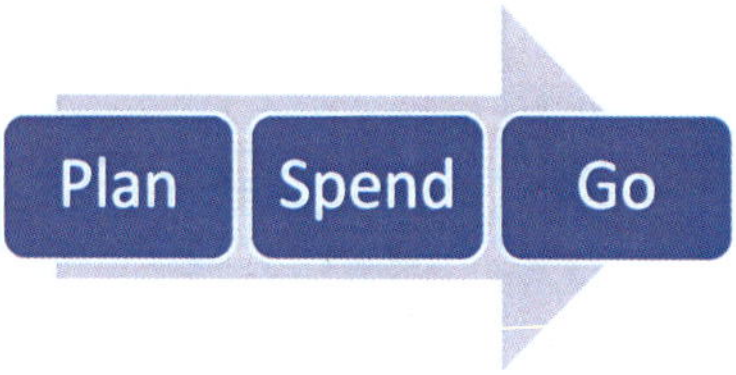

Running out of money (Reactive Approach)

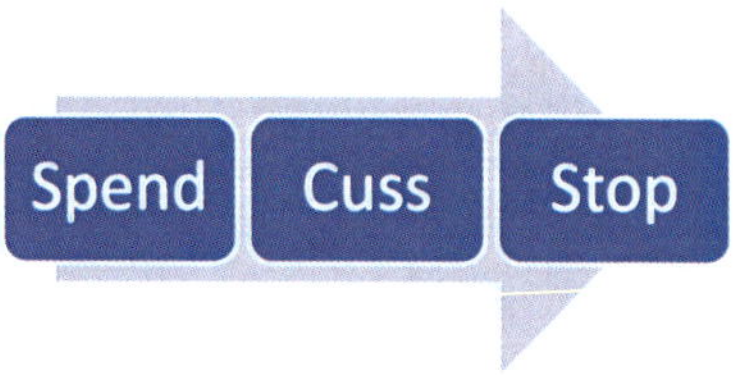

Net income is an individual's income after taking taxes and deductions into account. It is the check you take home after your company has deducted taxes, insurance, social security, etc.

Gross income – also known as gross pay when it's on a paycheck – is the individual's total pay from their employer before taxes or other deductions. It consists of income from wages and salary plus other forms of income, including pensions, alimony, interest, dividends, and rental income.

I don't know if you have had a similar experience, but when somebody asks me how much money I make, I tend to tell them my **gross income**, but in reality, it is my **net income**, the actual amount I have at my disposal to cover my expenses, that counts. As you can see in the example below, the money at your disposal to cover your expenses is $350 and not $500.

Gross weekly pay = $500
minus taxes
minus social security
minus health insurance
minus 401K

Net weekly pay = $350

Tip

Do not confuse your gross income with your net income. It is very important to understand the difference between the two.

Now that I knew I was short $1,000, I was in a dilemma – I had to either say goodbye to some of my expenses ☹

(hopefully not my VW Beetle – I love my Bug) or create some money instantaneously (how do I do that without robbing a bank?).

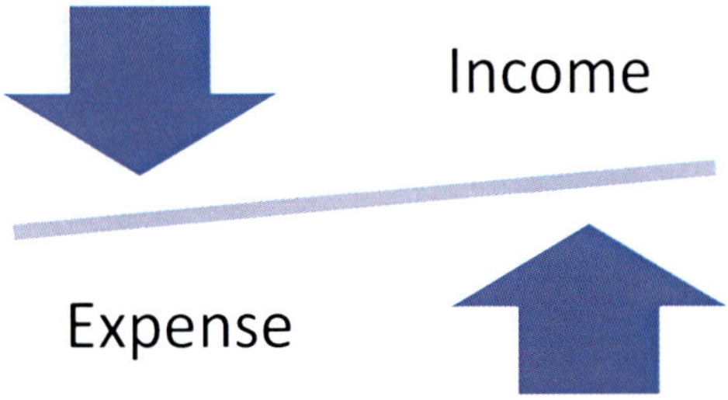

I sat there contemplating my options. Creating money without robbing a bank wasn't going to be easy, so my only other choice was to eliminate some of my expenses, without losing my favorite car and keeping a roof over my head. I sure seemed to have my priorities right. Although it's easy to joke about it now after five years; at the time I was devastated.

In all seriousness, I scrutinized my list of expenses with a fine-tooth comb. Here is an example of how my emergency budget morphed. (These are not my real numbers; I have simplified it for illustration purposes, but you will get the gist of it.)

Step 1 - I compared my previous financial situation with my current one.

Before divorce (2 incomes)	After divorce (1 income)
Total net income = $3600 (his-$2000, mine-$1600)	My net income - $1600
Expense	Expense
Mortgage - $1600	Mortgage - $1600
House Maintenance - $200	House Maintenance - $50
Utilities - $440 (includes his cell phone)	Utilities - $340
Car loan - $500 (his-$300, mine-$200)	Car loan - $200
Auto insurance - $120 (his-$70, mine-$50)	Auto insurance - $50
Gas - $120 (for both of us)	Gas - $60
Grocery - $300 (for both of us)	Grocery - $150
Restaurants - $150 (for both of us)	Restaurants - $50
Pocket money - $400 (his-$300, mine-$100)	My pocket money - $100
Total Expense = $3830	Total Expense = $2600
Surplus/Shortage = -$230	Surplus/Shortage = -$1000

As you can see above, even if our combined income before our divorce was more than double, our expenses were still higher than our income by $230, since we lived beyond our means. Thanks to my ex-husband's bad money-spending habits, we were always in the negative and charged things on our credit cards that we could not afford. We are under the impression that people making high salaries are rich, but if they spend recklessly and buy fancy cars and houses, they cannot afford by taking loans, then they are as poor as a person making an average salary. I explain the difference between a rich person and a wealthy person in Chapter 5.

Example:

House Maintenance ($200) - My ex-husband had a bad habit of starting house projects and not finishing them. Does that sound familiar to some of you? He would get all excited, make a list of things he needed from Home Depot, and off he went; however, when it came time to returning things he hadn't used, he would say, "I will do that later. I might need it again." And of course, later never came, nor would he use the items again, and worst of all, he wouldn't even finish the project.

His Pocket Money ($300) - He always wanted something or other – fancy computer gadgets, latest cell phone, new sunglasses, etc. You get the picture of where I am going with this. There was no end to it, and it was always the same story – "It's on sale" or "I am getting two for the price of one" or "It's only $50."

That's how we got into debt. A few dollars here and there adds up really quickly, especially if you cannot afford it. In the next chapter, we will discuss how to manage your debt.

Tip

Don't live beyond your means. Plan a budget for your expenses and don't spend more money than you can afford.

Okay, enough about my ex-husband; could we focus on me now? We are still in the middle of figuring out how to close my $1,000 gap.

Step 2 – I broke down my expenses further to see where I could cut back on spending.

After divorce (1 income)
My net income - $1600

Expense	Notes
Mortgage - $1600	call mortgage company
House Maintenance - $50	
Utilities - $340	
Electricity - $175	disconnect appliance not being used
Cable/Internet - $105	don't need 200 channels
Cell phone - $60	
Car loan - $200	
Auto insurance - $50	
Gas - $60	
Grocery - $150	eat less, gaining too much weight
Restaurants - $50	cook at home more
My pocket money - $100	no more shopping, only window shopping

Total Expense = $2600
Surplus/Shortage = -$1000

I knew the first thing I had to do was to call the mortgage company, so I picked up the phone and dialed their number. It was crucial for me to understand what my options were since I did not have the full payment amount and it was past the due date. There is often terrible news on TV about how people get evicted from their homes if they miss a payment, and their house might be put on a **short sale** or into **foreclosure**. I wasn't about to take any chances with being evicted.

Foreclosure is the action of taking possession of a mortgaged property when the homeowner or the borrower of the mortgage fails to keep up their payments.

A **short sale** is a home that is available at a purchase price that is less than the amount owed by its current owner. The transaction benefits the bank by avoiding repossession of the home in foreclosure, which is expensive and time-consuming.

You won't believe how relieved I was after I hung up the phone with the mortgage representative. Here is the essence of my conversation:

Mortgage Representative: "How may I help you?"

I explained how because of my divorce, I wouldn't be able to afford my mortgage payment, and as I flipped in panic mode, I asked him, "What is the difference between foreclosure and short sale? I want to understand my options."

He took the time to explain the difference and answered all my questions patiently: "Miss Bhojwani, since your income was reduced due to divorce, you can apply for hardship."

"I can do what? What does applying for hardship mean?" I wasn't aware of such a thing.

He explained, "Mortgage companies like us offer hardship mortgage programs which involve modifying one or more terms of your current loan program, replacing the loan with a new one via refinancing, restructuring the payment schedule, or by helping you catch up with any missed payments."

Thanking him for the explanation, I asked, "How could I apply for the program?"

After explaining the process, he asked, "Would you like me to email you the application?" Once I approved, he continued to say, "If you have difficulty answering any of the questions, please call us between 8 am and 6 pm, Monday to Friday; have a good day."

With great relief, I applied for the hardship and kept my fingers crossed. A few weeks later, when I received the approval letter, I jumped with joy. My mortgage was modified and my payment was reduced by $600 a month to fit my new income. A huge burden was lifted off my shoulders. I no longer had to fear becoming homeless. Thank you, God!

Some things are better left to the experts. There is no shame in asking for help. You don't know what you don't know, so get educated. Knowledge is power.

Tip

If you cannot afford your payment, don't hesitate to call your mortgage company or your landlord to negotiate a temporary rent reduction in times of a crisis — be it a divorce or a pandemic. Why might they work with you? Because it's in their best interest to work with you than to lose you altogether. You can similarly negotiate with your bank, utility company, student loan provider, credit card company, car loan provider, etc.

My mortgage payment was my biggest concern and expense, which was 100% of my $1,600 income, leaving me nothing for covering any of my other expenses. By speaking with the representative and applying for the hardship mortgage program, it freed up $600, or 37.5% of my income. That was a huge break!

Tip

In my case, it was my mortgage; in your case, it might be your rent and the process may be somewhat different, but the need to take action is equally important. You might need to negotiate with your landlord for a temporary rent reduction, or you may have to consider getting a cheaper place to live. Don't hesitate to call your landlord if you can't afford your rent. They need you as much as you need them.

Now that I had my mortgage payment under control, I worked on reducing my utility expenses, and then kept going down the list.

Did I really need 200 cable channels? Did I need to spend $10 a month on the digital TV recording equipment for my second TV? Did I even need a second TV and its extra electricity expense?

Tip

Determine if your expense is a "need" or a "nice to have."

Example:

Need - For me, having a TV with the basic 10 channels was a need. Nowadays, people have cut cable costs completely and watch live-streaming TV on the internet.

Nice to have - I would love to have a wide variety of channels to watch, but I definitely didn't need 200 channels.

One at a time, I went through all my bills — cable, internet, phone, electricity, oil. I got rid of any fancy features and also made arrangements with the utility companies to put my bill on a budget plan wherever applicable. This way, I knew what bill amounts to expect in a month and could budget accordingly. It is easy to put some of the bills like cable, phone, and electricity on automatic payment every month without thinking about it, but when money is tight, especially in times like this, knowing where every dollar of yours goes matters.

Tip

Have better control over your money. Look at your monthly statements before you pay the bill, especially if you have them on automatic payment mode from your bank account. Some of the payments easily forgotten are subscriptions for magazines, chess club, health club, Hulu, Netflix, etc.

Look at all the other places you can cut your unnecessary expenses, especially during a pandemic crisis when you need to be on an emergency budget — coffee, donuts, take-out, movies and popcorn, gym, hairdresser, impulse shopping, bars, gas, Hulu, Netflix, etc. Put it through the litmus test of "need" versus "nice to have."

After divorce (1 income)
My net income - $1600

Expense	Notes
Mortgage - $1600	call mortgage company
House Maintenance - $50	
Utilities - $340	
Electricity - $175	disconnect appliance not being used
Cable/Internet - $105	don't need 200 channels
Cell phone - $60	
Car loan - $200	
Auto insurance - $50	
Gas - $60	
Grocery - $150	eat less, gaining too much weight
Restaurants - $50	cook at home more
My pocket money - $100	no more shopping, only window shopping
Total Expense = $2600	
Surplus/Shortage = -$1000	

After divorce (1 income)
My net income - $1600

Expense	Notes
Mortgage - $1000	reduced by $600
House Maintenance - $50	
Utilities - $195	reduced by $145
Electricity - $85	
Cable/Internet - $50	
Cell phone - $60	
Car loan - $200	
Auto insurance - $50	
Gas - $60	
Grocery - $100	reduced by $50
Restaurants - $30	reduced by $20
My pocket money - $50	reduced by $50
Total Expense = $1735	total reduction = $865
Surplus/Shortage = -$135	

By bringing all my expenses to the bare bones, I was able to reduce the expenses by an additional $265, leaving a shortage of $135. I had cut my expenses by a total of $865, which is a whopping 54%. Imagine waking up tomorrow and seeing your expenses reduced by 54%; it will make you dance with joy.

Step 3 - I had to find a way to increase my income.

I began scratching my head to come up with a minimum of $135 more each month in order to cover all my expenses. Suddenly a light bulb went off; I grabbed my paycheck and saw that I was contributing 26% toward my **401(k) plan**. When I joined the company back in 2011, I had to tell HR how much I wanted to contribute, so I instructed them to take 18% out of my paycheck before taxes. I also asked them to automatically increase my contribution by 2% every year. Knowing myself, I am pretty sure I wouldn't have remembered to increase the **contribution** on my own, even if I knew it was the right thing to do. In 2012, HR took out 20% from my paycheck and the following year another 2%. By the time I divorced in 2015, they were taking out 26% from my paycheck. It was the best move I had ever made in terms of growing my retirement funds at a faster pace.

A **401(k) plan** is a tax-advantaged plan, which is a company-sponsored retirement account. Employees can make **contributions** to their 401(k) accounts through automatic payroll withholding. Employers may also make matching contributions.

Tip

I talk about reducing my contribution to the 401(k) plan because that is what I had with my company, but you may have other types of retirement plans like a **403(b) plan** or an **IRA plan** from which you could temporarily reduce your contribution.

A **403(b) plan**, also known as a tax-sheltered annuity plan, is a retirement plan for certain employees of public schools, employees of certain Code Section 501(c)(3) tax-exempt organizations, and certain ministers.

An **IRA plan** is an investment account that individuals may establish through a broker to save for retirement. It is a tax-advantaged investing tool.

Thanks to automation, where money is automatically transferred from one bank account to another (I explain how it works in great length in Chapter 4), and the power of **compound interest**, I had accumulated a good chunk of money in my retirement fund in a short period of time. I knew my ex-husband had an eye on it and I was afraid he would ask for a portion of it, but thankfully he didn't. I know what you are thinking, but don't jump to any conclusions; he is no saint, and trust me when I say he took more than his share of money in plenty of other ways.

> **Compound interest** is the addition of interest to the principal sum of a loan or deposit, or in other words, interest on interest. It is the result of reinvesting interest, rather than paying it out, so that interest in the next period is then earned on the principal sum plus previously accumulated interest.

If you remember in Chapter 1, we had discussed "What do you need to do differently while creating a budget versus an emergency budget?" In the comparison chart we saw that if you are following a budget, you need to grow your retirement fund, and if you are building an emergency fund, you need to temporarily reduce your contribution or sell unwanted things from your house to generate more income.

Tip

Make sure you are not selling things you will need later and have to replace at a higher price. Be smart about it and sell only unwanted things.

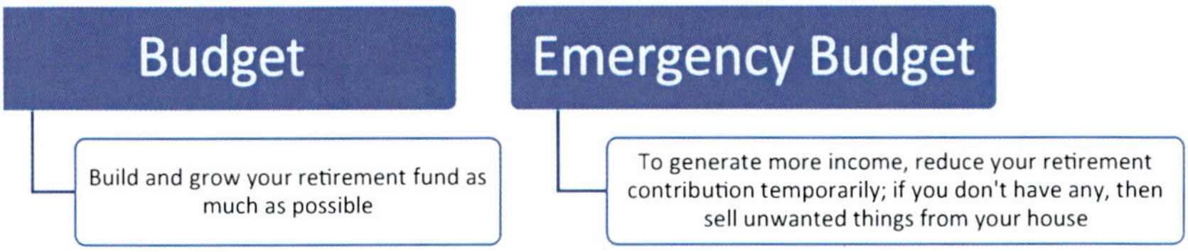

Since I was in a pandemic crisis and following an emergency budget, I reduced my 401(k) contribution from 26% to 6%, which increased my take-home pay by $320. Why 6% and not 0%? My company was doing a **matching contribution** of up to a maximum of 6%. In essence, when I was contributing 6% or $96 toward my 401(k) plan, they were also contributing an additional $96, thus my retirement fund was growing twice as fast. It would have been foolish of me not to take advantage of this golden opportunity. Who doesn't like free money?

A **matching contribution** is a type of contribution an employer chooses to make to his or her employee's employer-sponsored retirement plan. The contribution is based on elective deferral contributions that the employee makes.

Example:

Would you go to McDonalds and refuse to take the second McMuffin when they offer "a buy one get one free deal"? No, you wouldn't miss out on the free food. Who doesn't get the satisfaction of beating the system? You got something for free! Then why are you ready to give up free money at work, when your company is willingly offering you free money by matching your retirement plan contribution, or offering to pay for your education? It makes no sense whatsoever.

Here is how it works. If you contribute 6% or $96 from your salary and your company is matching 6%, then your money is growing by 12% or $192. You are losing out on $96 worth of free money every paycheck by not contributing.

Tip

Always contribute at least the percentage your company is matching in your retirement fund so you can take advantage of the faster growth rate.

Reducing my contribution by 20% solved my money shortage problem. My net income increased by $320 and not only did I have sufficient money to cover all my expenses (remember, I was short $135), but I got an additional $185 to add to my emergency fund. It felt like Christmas.

Gross weekly pay
minus taxes
minus social security
minus health insurance
minus 401K - REDUCED

Net weekly pay - INCREASED

Tip

If you are short on money to cover your bare-bone expenses, then consider reducing your contribution to your retirement fund temporarily, but make sure to increase the contribution back to where it was, plus some if possible, as soon as you get back on your feet, after the pandemic crisis is over. Promise me you will do that. And if you don't have any retirement fund, then sell unwanted things from your house.

Action Steps during Pandemic Crisis Budgeting

1) Jot down your gross and net income on a piece of paper.
2) Do a comparison of your financial situation before the pandemic and after.
3) Negotiate with stakeholders like bankers, landlords, utility companies, etc.
4) Follow an emergency budget by cutting all unnecessary expenses.
5) Find creative ways of increasing your income, like reducing your retirement fund contribution or selling unwanted things from your house.

Chapter 3

Begin the Countdown to Being Debt-Free

It doesn't matter if you make $20,000, $50,000 or $100,000 a year, it is your money-spending habits that either make you or break you. I showed you an example in Chapter 2 of how my ex-husband and I were in the negative (because we lived beyond our means) even though our combined income was $3,600 a month or $43,200 a year; this was more than double what I made by myself after the divorce, which was $1,600 a month or $19,200 a year.

One day when I came home from work, my ex-husband was all smiles and said to me, "Reshma, I have ordered a pair of Cocoons sunglasses and a UV-protection shirt, so when we go to the beach, I won't need to apply sunscreen lotion all over my body. I also ordered you this cute little sun hat with a wide brim, you will love it. It was 50% off since the bill was over $75. I charged it on the Visa card, the shipment will be here in two days." He sheepishly left the room before giving me a chance to speak, as he knew he would get a mouthful from me if he continued standing there.

Beats me why he needed all those UV-protection clothes. We had never been to the beach since we were married, nor did he take me after he bought the clothes. I don't think he wore that shirt even once; it just lay there in his closet.

While we were married, my ex-husband and I constantly argued about money, since our values were the complete opposite – he was a spender and I was a saver. Now that we are talking about it, I think our conversations turned into arguments at least once a month. Here is how our conversations started: he would be surfing the internet and call me over with, "Reshma, come here for a minute. I want to show you something." When I got to his desk, he would say, "Look at this four-pack printer ink cartridge; it's on sale for only 80 bucks."

With a puzzled look I asked him, "Don't we already have two of them sitting on the shelf?"

He replied, "Yes, but they don't go bad. Normally they cost over $100, plus they are offering free shipping."

I asked, "Do we need to spend the $80 this month? It's not that we will be using it anytime soon. You just bought a wireless keyboard and a mouse two weeks ago."

"Oh, come on, the keyboard and mouse were only 20 bucks." You could hear the annoyance in his voice. Then he went back to saying, "The cartridge for 80 bucks is a steal. I am surprised HP is offering it so cheap."

Not buying into his talk, I said, "I am sure they will offer another good deal again. It is a marketing gimmick to attract people like you. You have charged enough on the credit card this month. I would rather you not spend the extra money if you don't need the cartridges right away."

He banged his hand on the desk and said, "You sound as though I spend hundreds of dollars every month shopping. It's only 80 bucks; we not going to go broke spending $80. We make plenty of money."

I could feel my blood boiling, "Every dollar counts, but I don't expect you to understand, as you have no value for money. At the rate you spend, it is just a matter of time before we do actually go broke. We already have $20,000 in debt. Isn't that enough?"

He had the audacity to say, "Why are you making this such a big issue? Everybody in America has debt. It's normal; we are not the only family. An average American family has more than $50,000 in debt, and ours is only $20,000. We are in a much better shape than others."

That did it for me, and I lashed out, "Could be, but I'd rather have no debt and $20,000 in savings. You need to change your bad money-spending habits and stop adding more to our debt."

He gave me a dirty look, got up from his desk, and slammed the door shut as he left the room.

Our conversations always turned into arguments and our money problems were left unresolved. I was fed up with his behavior.

In 2014 Amy, a house cleaner, came to our house twice a week for an hour or two to help out. We paid her $10 an hour, and when we interviewed her, she said that she needed the job to make ends meet. However, she spent as though she had all the money in the world. I seldom saw her enter our house without a cup of Dunkin' Donuts coffee in her hand. We say, it's only $2, what's the big deal, but if you do the math, it's 20% of her hourly pay.

Example:

Let's assume she buys coffee five times a week from Dunkin' Donuts. It means she is spending $10 a week or $40 a month on coffee alone. That $40 could have covered her prepaid phone bill, instead of her always telling me that she didn't have enough balance in her phone to make a call.

Don't even get me started on needing money to buy cigarettes. One morning she came to work in shambles and asked me if I could pay her $10 in advance, as she was going to work for two hours that day. When I asked her if everything was all right, she said, "Yes, everything is fine, but could I please have $10?"

Looking at her state, I thought something serious had happened and gave her the money. She took it and while running out the door said, "I'll be right back." She returned in ten minutes with a cup of Dunkin' Donuts coffee and a packet of cigarettes in her hand. With cigarettes being almost $10 a pack, it was beyond my comprehension as to how she could afford such an expensive habit.

I couldn't believe my eyes; this was her emergency? For the last ten minutes I had been wondering if everything was all right with her, and she came back grinning from ear to ear now that she had her fix of caffeine and nicotine.

I could not for the life of me understand why a person who didn't have a dime in her pocket would want to spend $2 on Dunkin' Donuts coffee, when it can be made at home for a few cents a cup.

Tip

I can't tell you enough. Don't live beyond your means and stop spending more than you can afford. Every dollar counts.

My ex-husband fell into the same category as Amy of having bad spending habits. He too had the expensive habit of smoking. I don't know how often Amy bought cigarettes, but my ex-husband smoked a pack a day, which at $10 a pack added up to $300 a month, $3,600 a year, amounting to $36,000 in ten years. We could have bought a brand spanking new car with that much money.

Whenever he wanted something, he would justify it by saying it costs only $5, only $20, only $100, only $500.

Guess what the outcome was? Over the years, all his "nice to have" expenses, including his cigarettes, kept being charged on the credit card, and before we knew it, we were $10,000 in debt that we could not afford to pay.

So what did we do? We paid only the minimum due and the huge interest rates every month, and our debt kept increasing by $2,000-$3,000 every year. Just before our divorce, it had reached as high as $50,000, and I got stuck with half of it as part of the settlement agreement. He did the spending, and I got punished. I felt like strangling him.

When I started my financial coaching business, one of my clients, Leslie, was frustrated because she had accumulated $8,000 in debt over the past ten years. She said she religiously paid the minimum due every month, but her debt amount didn't seem to budge, even though she mostly paid it down and sometimes charged more again. I am sure you can relate. I definitely can, as I had been in her shoes for several years.

Let me demonstrate why your debt doesn't seem to budge by doing some math. I know what you are thinking. No more math please, I hate math. But bear with me for a minute; after all, this is a finance book.

You made a purchase of $500 on your credit card and did not pay it all off when you received the bill. Instead, you paid only the minimum due of $25. Next month you were expecting to see a bill for $475 ($500-$25); however, you got a bill for $481, and you scratch your head. Why is it $6 more? It's because you have a 15% interest rate (in this example) on your card. The same thing happened the following month. You paid only the minimum due of $25, expected a bill for $456 ($481-$25), but got a bill for $462. That's how the credit card company gets you. You get stuck in the loop because of the interest charges and late fees.

Tip

When following an emergency budget during a pandemic crisis, make every effort to pay at least the minimum to stay afloat, so that you can keep as much money on hand to cover your bare-bone expenses (unless you have made some special arrangements with the credit card company).

After the pandemic crisis is over, when you go back to following a budget, always pay more than the minimum due on your credit card to get ahead in the game, and pay off your debts at a faster pace. I will explain how the debt snowball method works later in the chapter. I learnt this very effective method from Dave Ramsey, one of the well-known leaders in the industry.

If you want a refresher on "What do you need to do differently while creating a budget versus an emergency budget," go back and read Chapter 1 and refer to the comparison chart.

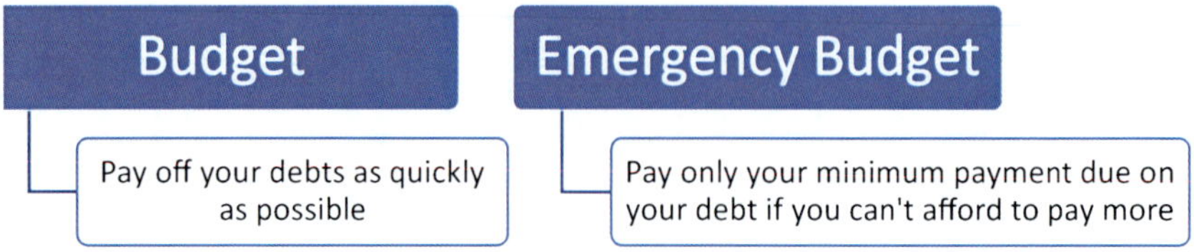

As the years went by, my ex-husband and I charged vacations, furniture, etc. on our credit cards. Our $10,000 in debt soon increased to $25,000 and eventually reached $50,000. As a saver, I hated being in debt, so I focused on paying it off as much as possible. On the other hand, my ex-husband thought we were in good shape. According to him, the average American has way more than $50,000 in debt. "Savings" was a foreign word to him; he didn't even have a savings account before he met me. Over the years, we yo-yo'ed between $25,000 and $50,000 in debt several times.

By the time we divorced, I was an expert in reducing our debt, and paid off $25,000 (my portion of our debt) within three years. I have been debt-free since then. Are you wondering what may have happened to my ex-husband's portion of $25,000 in debt? Your guess is as good as mine.

How does the debt snowball method work?

First make a list of all your debts, from the smallest to the largest. Then pay only the minimum payment due on all your debts except the one with the smallest balance; pay as much as possible on the smallest one.

Once you pay your smallest balance off in full, roll the money you were paying on that debt into the debt with the next smallest balance. This way, you gain momentum as you knock out each balance. Keep repeating the process until you are debt-free.

Example:

Let me show you how you can eliminate $7,400 in debt with a $400 a month budget in 19 months with the debt snowball method.

List of debts from smallest to largest (Budget = $400 for this example)

DEBT	AMT	MIN	PAY	NOTES
Visa	$400	$25	$200	pay max until paid in full
Mastercard	$2000	$60	$60	pay min.
Car Loan	$5000	$140	$140	pay min.
TOTAL	$7400			

After 2 months

DEBT	AMT	MIN	PAY	NOTES
Visa	$0	$0	$0	has been paid in full :)
Mastercard	$1880	$60	$260	pay min + $200 (Visa pay amt)
Car Loan	$4720	$140	$140	pay min.
TOTAL	$6600			

After another 8 months

DEBT	AMT	MIN	PAY	NOTES
Mastercard	$0	$0	$0	has been paid in full :)
Car Loan	$3600	$140	$400	pay min + $260 (Mastercard pay amt)
TOTAL	$3600			

After another 9 months

YOU ARE DEBT FREE. CONGRATULATIONS!

As you can see in the example above, we were able to become debt-free in 19 months with a $400 budget. If you can make some temporary sacrifices, like eating out less often, making fewer runs to Dunkin' Donuts and putting more than $400 toward your debt payment, you will be able to eliminate $7,400 even sooner than 19 months. You are in control of your destiny.

Tip

If you follow the method with discipline, you will be debt-free before long. This method is very effective and I can tell you firsthand that it works. I was able to eliminate $25,000 in three years, and I am confident you will also be able to, if you put your mind to it.

Action Steps to Pay Off your Debt

1) Do not spend what you cannot afford.
2) If you are in debt, stop making new purchases on your credit card.
3) Make a budget to pay off your debt and stick to it.
4) Use the debt snowball method as discussed in this chapter.
5) Cut your expenses wherever you can and pay toward your debt.

Chapter 4

Treat Your Emergency Fund Like Autopilot

When I moved from Florida to Connecticut, I decided to go with a different bank. As I entered the bank, I was asked to wait for the account manager while he was attending to another customer. Within ten minutes, the manager escorted the customer out of his office, turned toward me, and signaled me to step into his office. "Please have a seat. What can I do for you today?"

"I want to open a personal checking and savings account, but I don't want to pay any monthly service fees."

He smiled and said, "Don't worry about that; there are ways to go around it. First, you need to provide me with some personal information to get you started." He then opened an online form on his computer, turned the screen toward me so I could see what he was typing and bombarded me with questions regarding my name, address, phone number, social security number, company name, job details, income, etc.

Once he finished gathering all the information he needed, he said, "Since you don't need any bells and whistles, we can open a basic 'Everyday Checking' account for you. It does have a $10 monthly service fee, but it can be waived if you ask your workplace to do a direct deposit of your salary into your account."

"The 'Everyday Checking' account works for me. I am sure my company will be able to do a direct deposit."

"I will explain how everything works before you leave. Now, as for your savings account, I recommend the 'Way2Save Savings' account. It's a great way to save automatically and build your savings. It has a minimum opening deposit of $25. It comes with a feature called 'Save As You Go Transfers' where we'll transfer $1 of your funds from your linked checking account to your Way2Save Savings account whenever you make a non-recurring debit card purchase."

"I've had several savings accounts over the years in different banks, but I have never heard of an automatic transfer feature before. I already love it."

The manager proudly explained, "It's a new product in our bank and has become very popular. It's only a dollar, but it adds up to a substantial amount very quickly."

"I can imagine that. I am sure there is a monthly service fee for providing such a neat feature."

With a sheepish look, he replied, "Yes, there is a $5 fee, but it will be waived if you set up monthly automatic transfers of $25 or more to reach your savings goals. We have great reviews from customers about this feature. They all love it since they are now saving much more than they would have if they were left to their own devices."

My eyes widened and I said, "I can see how this automation can empower savings. It brings in discipline without having to actually put any effort toward remembering to set aside money every month. It also gives peace of mind, since you are being smart about building your emergency fund, which in my opinion everybody should have, with at least a $1,000 in it."

The manager nodded his head in agreement and said, "You're right, I would recommend $1,000 at the minimum, although being able to cover three to six months of expenses would be even better. You never know when an unplanned expense comes up, like a car repair, medical bill, water pump breakdown, losing your job. Would you like me to open the 'Way2Save Savings' account for you?"

"That will be great, and could you please set up my account to transfer $100 on the first of every month. I want to get into the good habit of saving by paying myself first, before I even spend a dollar on anything else. This way I can no longer make the excuse of not having anything left to save at the end of the month."

Smiling, the manager said, "Good thinking; you seem to be very financially savvy, and I wish there were more people like you. It is sad to say, but a lot of our customers are clueless about how much money they have in their accounts. As far as '**paying yourself first'** goes, they don't even know what that means." He finished setting up both my accounts and gave me all the paperwork and instructions. I thanked him and left the bank feeling very satisfied.

> **Paying yourself first** means to put money away in your savings account before you spend anything. Saving comes first, not last.

How "paying yourself first" works:

Pay yourself first (save first)	Don't pay yourself (save last)
net weekly pay = $350	net weekly pay = $350
minus put in savings = $25	disposable income = $350
disposable income = $325	minus expenses = $348
minus expenses = $325	balance remaining = $2
balance remaining = $0	put in savings = $2
emergency fund = $25	emergency fund = $2

As seen in the example above, when you get your paycheck, pay yourself first by putting $25 into your savings account. What's left is what you have to pay bills, your rent, and all your other expenses. This ensures that you make routine savings contributions. You may not have anything left at the end of the month, but as you can see, your emergency fund is growing at a faster pace.

When you didn't pay yourself first, you had only $2 left at the end to put into savings. What do you think happened to the additional $23? You probably spent it in a restaurant or did some impulse shopping.

It didn't take long for my savings to grow. Within six months I was able to reach my goal of saving a $1,000 in my emergency fund. Opening the "Way2Save Savings" account was the greatest thing since sliced bread. You must be wondering how it grew to a $1,000 when I had scheduled to transfer only $100 a month. Here is how I did it:

Step 1 - $100 was automatically transferred every first of the month.

Step 2 - Every time I used my debit card to make a purchase, like filling up gas, buying groceries, paying at a restaurant, etc., $1 was automatically transferred from my checking account to my savings account. This turned out to be a more powerful tool than I had anticipated. Whenever I would check my bank statement at the end of the month, I would expect an additional $100 in my saving, but there was always an additional $110 or so, which meant I used my debit card a minimum of ten times during the month.

Step 3 - At the end of every month, I manually transferred an additional $60 into my savings account. That's the amount I had left over in my miscellaneous expense bucket, which I rarely used, after taking care of all my expenses.

Step 4 - **The power of automation** - In one month, $110 was automatically being saved, without any effort from me. I had to intentionally save an additional $60 per month to meet my $1,000 goal. Having an automated system in place definitely helped me achieve my goal faster. If you do the math, it adds up to $1,020.

Step 5 - **Manual process** - Would I have saved $170 every month had I been left to my own devices? I doubt it, but did I have the discipline to save $60 a month and transfer it to my savings account manually? Yes, because in my mind it was less daunting and more achievable.

My point is, saving money does not need to be a complicated process. Although automation or paying yourself first has magical results, it is not magic. It is more about the mindset of a person. If the first thing you do is automatically transfer the money to a savings account before you even see it in your checking account, it works as though that money never existed (out of sight, out of mind). You adapt to work with what you have and make it work for you.

Tip

Always pay yourself first and automate your savings process.

Another way of automating your saving is by asking your workplace to directly deposit a percentage of your salary into a savings account, even if it is only 1%. As you have seen from my explanation above, every dollar counts.

Inflation is the general increase in prices and fall of the purchasing value of money.

Example:

Every year I received a 2% to 3% salary increase from my company to keep pace with **inflation**, but instead of increasing my spending, I increased my saving and bumped up the automatic transfer amount from $100 to $300 to $500. Why? Because the additional income went straight toward my savings before I ever saw it. By doing so, even though my salary increased, the amount I received in hand did not change.

I talked about how I eliminated my $25,000 in debt in three years in Chapter 3. Once my debts were paid off, I was able to bump up the automatic transfer amount to $1,000. After that, my money started growing exponentially and I was able to dream for the first time in my life.

Not only did I save $1,000 in my emergency fund, but I also grew it to a point where I had sufficient money to cover my expenses for three to six months, and thanks to this, I slept like a baby every night.

Now that I have my emergency fund in place to my comfort level, I am able to save toward my goal of buying a rental property. Becoming debt-free was a life-changing moment for me and it opened doors I couldn't have dared to dream of while in debt.

Before Pandemic 2020 - I had set up my automated transfer amount to $1,000 to save toward the 20% down payment I need to buy my first rental property.

During Pandemic 2020 - During these uncertain days, and because my income has been affected, I have lowered the automated transfer amount to the minimum requirement of $25. I know it is not that simple, but in times like this, we need to learn to adapt.

After Pandemic 2020 - First I will replenish my three-to-six-months emergency fund and then resume saving toward my rental property goal.

The beauty of having an emergency fund is that during a pandemic crisis (and there will always be a crisis of some kind or another on the horizon) money is tight, but I am not in panic mode and feel blessed. It breaks my heart to see so many people around me suffering because they are struggling to make ends meet.

Tip

To reiterate, if you are following the emergency budget during a pandemic crisis, then use your emergency fund sparingly.

We discussed the chart below in-depth in Chapter 1.

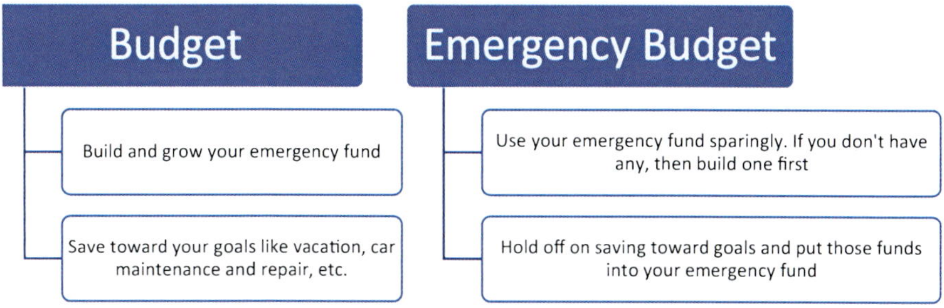

This pandemic in 2020 may be a setback, but when all is said and done, we will come out stronger than ever before.

Action Steps to Pay Yourself First

1) Open a savings account (if you don't already have one).
2) Pay yourself first.
3) Automate your savings – you could do either (a) or (b), whichever works better for you.

a) Work with your bank to schedule an automatic transfer of money from your checking to your savings account.
b) Work with your company to direct deposit a portion of your paycheck into your savings account.

Chapter 5

With Knowledge, Create Your Own Silver Spoon

I would rather be wealthy than rich. You must be thinking – what are you talking about? They both mean the same thing – having a great deal of money or assets. Even though on the surface they look the same, when you dig deeper, there is a big difference in the two words, especially when it comes to the financial mindset of a **rich person** versus a **wealthy person**.

> The difference between a **wealthy person** and a **rich person** is that a **wealthy person** will always be wealthy, whereas a **rich person** will be rich only for a short period of time until the money is gone.

What does being wealthy mean?

Wealth is the accumulation of assets. Wealthy people save 15% or more of their paycheck, have little debt, and live well within their means. We discussed the importance of living within our means in Chapter 3. Since they don't have flashy lifestyles, we might not even recognize wealthy people when we meet them. The most important distinction is that a wealthy person has a high **net worth**.

Net worth is the value of all assets, minus the total of all liabilities. To put another way, net worth is what is owned minus what is owed.

What does being rich mean?

Being rich simply means having a high income. Even though the rich may have a lot of money, it doesn't make them wealthy because they also spend a lot. Instead of saving (as the wealthy do), they buy expensive cars and jewelry and often need to use loans for it. You might see people driving brand new BMWs, but that doesn't mean that they have a fat bank account.

Who do you think has more money? (This is not a trick question.)

John makes $250,000 per year and spends $225,000. On the other hand, Mark makes $80,000 per year and saves half of it.

If your answer is Mark, then you are correct.

John	Mark
Income - $250,000	Income - $80,000
Expense -$225,000	Expense -$40,000
Savings - $25,000	Savings - $40,000

Example:

I was richer before my divorce when my ex-husband and I were bringing in two incomes from our separate jobs. However, the money lasted for only a short period of time because we lived beyond our means; in fact, we always had a negative balance. You can refer to the comparison charts of my income and expenses before divorce and after divorce in Chapter 2.

After the divorce, even though my income ($1,600) was less than half of what my ex-husband and I made combined ($3,600), due to my good money habits and being more of a saver than a spender, my money started growing exponentially, and I started accumulating wealth. I first got rid of my $25,000 debt in three years by applying the debt snowball method. I explained how that works in Chapter 3.

I then built an emergency fund by saving surplus money, once I paid off my debts in full. Thanks to the power of automation, I have six months' worth of expenses in my emergency fund. You can read about it in Chapter 4.

I began saving toward a 20% down payment for a rental property. Unfortunately, I had to put it on hold when I switched to an emergency budget during the coronavirus pandemic. I will resume it again once I am back on a budget, when this pandemic crisis is all said and done. You can refer to Chapter 1 if you need a refresher on the difference between a budget and an emergency budget.

In a nutshell, I was richer before my divorce with a higher combined income; however, I am wealthier today than I have ever been, and I actually have a positive **net worth** for the first time in my life, despite having a lower single income.

Does this mean you can become a millionaire if you develop the mindset of a millionaire? The answer is, "You absolutely can and will become a millionaire" if you make it your goal and put your heart and mind into it. Remember, the key is to save more and spend less.

How do you develop the mindset of a millionaire? By changing your financial mindset, which is your predetermined set of beliefs about money; you just may need to replace it with a new one. Money is rarely about money; in fact, it is all about behavior – your habits, thoughts, and feelings about money are going to determine how you spend and what your financial goals will be.

How would you describe a rich person? The first thing that comes to mind is someone with a lot of money who is quite showy with it – driving fancy cars, living in a fancy house, wearing fancy clothes and eating at fancy restaurants, right? Does this mean they are wealthy too? Not so fast; not if they are living beyond their means and are up to their eyeballs in debt.

On the flip side, wealthy people drive used cars, live in average neighborhoods, wear average-priced clothes and are very careful with their money. Rich people only have money, but wealthy people have knowledge and **financial literacy**.

> **Financial literacy** is the ability to understand and effectively apply various financial skills, including personal financial management, budgeting, and investing. It helps individuals become self-sufficient so that they can achieve financial stability.

Do you want to look rich or do you want to be wealthy? With the mindset of a millionaire you can be one of those people who are genuinely wealthy, rather than someone who spends a lot of money but has very little in the bank. The ball is in your court.

"Rich" girl's shopping bill	"Wealthy" girl's shopping bill
sweater - $250	sweater - $65
purse - $5000	purse = $0
pants - $300	pants - $45
boots - $500	boots - $50
net worth - $15,000	net worth - $1.2 million

Action Steps to Start Building Wealth

1) Stop living beyond your means.
2) Cut your expenses to the bare bones.
3) Save a minimum of $1,000 in your emergency fund (if you haven't already).
4) Pay off your debt.
5) Save at least 15% or more.

Chapter 6

Make Money While You Sleep - Millionaires Do It, Why Not You?

In January of 2019, I called a friend and asked him if we could meet for lunch. We met at Olive Garden at noon the following day and sat at a booth. I ordered bread and water. Just kidding!

He asked me, "What's going on? You look so chirpy today, have you won the lottery?"

"No, but I made my last payment toward my $25,000 debt yesterday. I am finally debt-free."

He gave me a high five and said, "That's fantastic. You go, girl!"

With a big smile, I said, "Thanks, that's a weight off my shoulders!"

"Now that you won't have a credit card payment next month, have you thought about what you are going to do with the surplus money you will have at your disposal?" I shook my head no, so he continued, "I recommend investing in real estate and buying rental property so you can make passive income."

I gave him a blank stare. "What is passive income?"

He explained, "Passive income is money you earn in a way that requires little to no effort to earn and maintain, like rental property, business investments, writing a book, or building a blog."

I stopped eating my soup and looked up at him with a curious smile. "You mean I won't need to work to make money? When people say 'make money while you sleep', are they referring to passive income? How does it work? Do I need to stay in bed more often?"

Seeing me get all excited, he laughed and said, "Don't be silly, read the book '*Rich Dad Poor Dad*' by Robert Kiyosaki. He does a good job explaining the advantages of investing in real estate and how passive income works. Well, I have to head back to the office. Congratulations again for your great accomplishment. Paying off your debt in three years is no small feat; it requires a lot of discipline. You should feel proud of yourself." I thanked him and we walked out together.

I took my friend's advice and read the book, and it blew my mind. Why don't they teach this stuff in school? Why are we encouraged to earn only **linear income** by doing a job? If everybody had multiple streams of income, then nobody would be stressed about money and stuck **living paycheck to paycheck.**

> **Linear income,** also known as active income, is the income a person receives from the work they do. For this, one needs to put in a certain number of hours every week as work. The linear income stops when the person stops working. It requires continued work; this includes wages, tips, salaries, and commissions. It is also for self-employed and independent contractors.

That day was a turning point in my life. I made it my goal to stop **living paycheck to paycheck** and do whatever it takes to create multiple streams of income for myself. Today, I can stand tall and tell you that I am no longer living paycheck to paycheck and have sufficient money in my emergency fund to cover my expenses for six months, which lets me sleep like a baby at night (even during this coronavirus pandemic in 2020). I wrote about how I used the power of automation to save this money and the importance of paying yourself first in Chapter 4.

> **Living paycheck to paycheck** simply means you are using most or all of your monthly income to cover your monthly expenses, with no money left over and no money in savings.

By living within my means, spending less and saving more, I achieved two major goals in my life – one was paying off my debt, and the other was to stop living paycheck to paycheck. I am now working on my third goal, which is to be wealthy and build my net worth by having multiple streams of income and saving 15% or more. I explained the difference between being rich and wealthy, and the meaning of having the mindset of a millionaire in Chapter 5.

In her book '*Self Made*', Nely Galan says "Don't buy shoes, buy buildings." I love what it implies and have made it my motto. I am currently saving money for the 20% down payment to buy my first rental property, although I have put this on hold as I am on an emergency budget during the pandemic crisis of 2020. You can refer to the difference between a budget and an emergency budget in Chapter 1.

Research shows that self-made millionaires have at least three streams of income. This can be invaluable – not only for monetary value, but because it will allow you to live the life you want, and it will hedge against whatever the future might throw at you; for instance, the coronavirus pandemic of 2020.

This pandemic crisis is a perfect illustration of how people with a single source of linear income, which is the source of income for more than 90% of people around the world, have been affected. Millions of people have lost their jobs and are collecting unemployment. My point is, stop living paycheck to paycheck; have multiple streams of income and don't get caught off-guard again – there is always a looming crisis on the horizon.

Precisely for this reason, I have multiple streams of income. Since I make linear income in my financial coaching business, I strategically partnered with two other businesses – **LegalShield,** a company that provides affordable legal services, and **Primerica,** a financial services company. I selected these two companies because they are complementary to my coaching service and I can provide added value to my clients. It also generates passive income for me, so it is a win-win for both my clients and me.

How I came across LegalShield as a business opportunity:

When I started my financial coaching business, I needed a lawyer to create a contract document for me. As you know, lawyers cost an arm and a leg, so my friend recommended that I get a LegalShield plan. The way their plan works is that instead of paying a lawyer expensive hourly fees, the member pays a small monthly fee and gets access to experienced attorneys who can help with any legal issue. I became a member and was so impressed with their services that I decided to partner with them so I could help my clients gain access to affordable legal services too, while I make passive income.

Why I chose to partner with Primerica:

As a financial coach, I teach my clients how to save money, so that they can build their emergency funds, invest in retirement plans and other investment vehicles like mutual funds and exchange-traded funds (ETFs). Primerica offers life insurance and helps families with their investments; instead of referring my clients to other financial advisors, I have partnered with them so that I can directly help my clients, and also make passive income along the way with my connection with Primerica.

Tip

When choosing alternative sources of income, don't put all your eggs in the same basket. Don't work a second or third job that typically requires your active participation and is a source of linear income; instead, find sources of income that will generate **passive income**.

Evaluate your skills and your passion and find a side hustle or a part-time business you will enjoy. Even if you love what you do, I'm sure you wouldn't mind earning some extra income without the blood, sweat, tears, and time commitment of another job.

Some passive income ideas you could look into are renting out property, building a blog, writing a book or an e-book, writing a song, creating an online course or an automated webinar, network marketing, multilevel marketing (MLM), etc.

Passive income is money you earn in a way that requires little-to-no daily effort to maintain. It will take some work to get up and running, but it may eventually earn you money while you sleep.

Example of what my multiple streams of income look like:

Financial Coaching Income	Rental Property Income	Book Royalty Income	Legalshield (MLM and B2B) Income	Primerica Income
Short Term - Make linear income only when a service is provided to a client. Long Term - Make **residual income** if any profit remains after paying all expenses	Short term - Make passive income while paying off mortgage Long term - Make **residual income** once mortgage has been paid off	Short term - Make passive income until the book costs are recovered Long term - Make **residual income** once the book costs have been recovered	Short term -Associates start making linear income by making sales on their own. Short term - Once an associate gets the hang of it, they make passive income by building out a sales organization that can help them obtain more commission when they make sales. Long term - Associates collect additional **residual income** for each membership that lasts over a year.	Short term - Make linear income on life insurance sales Short term - Make passive income on sales made by your downline. Long term - make **residual income** on sales made in investment products

As seen in the example above, the common thread between all the sources of income is **residual income**. Generating residual income is one of the key factors in building wealth, but it doesn't happen overnight. You need to be patient. Wealthy people make money while they sleep, and so can you.

> **Residual income** is when you continue to get paid after the work is done. This includes royalties from books, movies, or songs, and income that comes from real estate or business investments where you don't actually have to be present to earn it.

Although the words "passive income" and "residual income" are used interchangeably in different industries, what I would like you to take away from this book is that there are different types of income, and you should strive to have multiple streams so you don't have financial stress when another pandemic crisis hits us in the future.

If you would like to know more about the different types of income or any other topics I have covered in this book, please feel free to contact me at **www.flourishbizcenter.com** or **reshmabhojwani1@gmail.com**. I will be more than happy to answer any of your questions. I am the founder of Flourish Bizcenter. I provide financial coaching services to help clients reduce their stress around money, organize their financial chaos, and stop living paycheck to paycheck. I teach them my system – so that they can reach their financial freedom goals in this lifetime.

"If you don't find a way to make money while you sleep, you will work until you die."

– Warren Buffett

Action Steps to Stop Living Paycheck to Paycheck

1) Evaluate your skills and find your passion.
2) Find alternative sources of income beyond what you earn from your regular job.
3) Have multiple streams of income.
4) Stop living paycheck to paycheck.
5) Build your net worth.

Epilogue

Stop Counting Sheep, Dream Financial Freedom

Ever since I was in my twenties, I've had this gut feeling that one day I would own my own business and travel the world. Today I can proudly say that "one day" has arrived, and I am an entrepreneur who owns several businesses. I am the founder of Flourish Bizcenter, providing financial coaching services; an author; a partner at LegalShield (an MLM and B2B company providing affordable legal services); a partner at Primerica (a financial services company); and I will be a real estate investor in the near future (once I have saved up my 20% down payment).

You must be curious to know if my intuition about traveling the world has come to fruition. Even though I have visited and lived in a few countries – Iran, India, the United States, South Africa, and England, I have not embarked on my world tour as of yet; however, I can feel that "one day" coming closer and closer. It does require a substantial amount of money and some planning.

Where am I going to get this "substantial amount of money," you might ask? It's baked into my **financial freedom** goals.

> **Financial freedom** is the freedom to quit your job to do something you love, even if you get paid less. It means that you get to make life decisions without being overly stressed about the financial impact because you are prepared. You control your finances instead of being controlled by your finances.

What are my financial freedom goals?

1) **Have financial security,** which means not living paycheck to paycheck, and not having to worry "how am I going to pay the bill?" if my hot water heater breaks down unexpectedly.
   How am I going to achieve this? By spending less and saving more. I need to grow my emergency fund to cover one year of my expenses. Today I can cover six months, so I am halfway there.
2) **To travel the world.**
   How am I going to achieve this? By having multiple streams of income where I can make money while I sleep, which will give me the freedom and time to travel. This is why I have set up several businesses.

3) **To own a Hummer;** isn't that bizarre? What can I say, a girl wants what a girl wants. I don't want a big mansion or a private jet, I just want my Hummer.

   How am I going to achieve this? By incorporating it into my budget and saving money using the power of automation in my "Hummer savings account."

Everybody has different visions and goals in life. Somebody may want to own a boat or a Corvette, someone else might want to make a million dollars or retire a whole decade early.

What are your financial freedom goals? Make a list of your goals and then plan to achieve them. I assure you that you can reach your financial freedom goals in this lifetime if you follow your budget consistently, develop the mindset of a millionaire, and have multiple streams of income to build your wealth.

Tip

You can achieve financial freedom in this lifetime if you make it your goal.

Actions Steps to Achieve your Financial Freedom Goals

1) Make a list of your income and expenses.
2) Create a budget or emergency budget as per your financial situation.
3) Live within your means, spend less and save more.
4) Save $1,000 in your emergency fund.
5) Eliminate your debt.
6) Build a 3-6 month emergency fund.
7) Save toward your goals by using the power of automation.
8) Develop the mindset of a millionaire and build your net worth.
9) Have multiple streams of income.
10) Make a list of your financial freedom goals and a plan to achieve them.

Acknowledgments

I have to start by thanking my awesome mom, Veena, for being patient with me while I neglected her and spent hours and hours every day in research and writing. She would remind me that it was nighttime and that I needed to go to bed, and made sure I ate on time and stayed hydrated.

I couldn't have published this book without the support of my wonderful writing coach, Michael Sharpe. I thank him for having faith in my writing ability and giving me the opportunity to write this first book. He taught me the ropes and stood by me throughout the process and made it seamless – right from the book's conception, to reading early drafts and providing priceless suggestions, to working with the copy editor and graphic artist, and submitting my book to the publisher. I feel honored to work with him and have him as my writing coach.

Mom and Michael, I thank you both from the bottom of my heart.